From

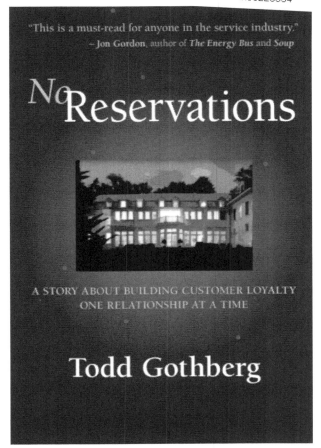

Pick up your copy today at Amazon.com!

Believe
By Todd Gothberg
Author of "No Reservations"

Several years ago I started a Faith & Fitness based blog, combining two of my life passions together in an effort to inspire people with my words and my example. I've been beyond blessed to have experienced both highs and lows in my life, and it's been God's unwavering guidance and presence through it all which inspired this devotional. I hope that the words provide comfort and assurance that you are not alone, and that most importantly, you are loved.

Todd M. Gothberg

Contents

Lessons from Louie

I've been through a lot in my life. And then I went through 2013's Boston Marathon. While I finished an hour before the blasts which tragically rocked a city, a nation, and a world, I found myself experiencing a range of emotions from the point I learned of the attacks until the second suspect was captured four days later. Shock. Sadness. Despair. Anger. Regret. Guilt. Relief. Peace. And while I was not physically impacted, I way underestimated the emotional toll Boston would take on me. Depression had parked itself in my soul. I know this is hard to believe, but I even found myself not wanting to run - the one "escape" I had gone to over the years to cope. My "therapy" became a reminder of what had gone terribly wrong just a few days earlier. Instead of basking in the glow of my 15th Boston finish, I was struggling to find purpose, passion and reason to move forward with life as I once knew it.

And then, as I added a few new books to my work library, I came across Laura Hillenbrand's "Unbroken" which I had read two years earlier and recalled meeting the man about whom the book was written. I met Louie Zamperini at Rev. Billy Graham's home in Montreat, NC; the book chronicles his incredible story of perseverance in the face of overwhelming odds and the brutally sadistic treatment by his Japanese captors during WW II. He told me that day that the key to survival and not being "broken" by his circumstances was the hope he held on to which displaced any fear, the dignity he maintained which kept his soul alive, and the conviction in his heart that everything happened for a reason - that in the end, it would all eventually come to good. Out of despair, out of tragedy, out of evil, out of hatred, eventually these things prevail: *Hope. Dignity. Conviction.* and *Love.* Louie had reminded me that day that just as with the death of Jesus Christ on the cross, my experience did not end that Monday with the death and despair at the finish line. The story was not complete. And while I couldn't change what had happened or what I had been through, I could change my outlook and my perspective moving forward. I could once again be the light that people were seeking in a dark world. I *needed* to be the light that people were seeking in a dark world. I needed to simply trust, and to Believe that death once again did not and would not have the final say.

"I have told you these things so that you may have peace. In this world you will have trouble. But take heart. I have overcome the world" - John 16:33

On Being a Man

I was honored to be asked by Jon Gordon to write a one-page letter to his son Cole, upon his 13th birthday, regarding what it means to be a man. My message follows....

Being a Man is about being love. If love is the single greatest commandment, and Christ is Love, then the qualities and characteristics described in 1 Corinthians 13:4-8 best describe how we as men should **be**. Not just *act*. Anyone can "act". Being is a core-thing. Acting is a surface-thing. Surface stuff never holds when the storms of life hit. So at the core, being a man is about **patience**. It's about knowing very often our timing won't be God's timing. That our prayers will always be answered, but not necessarily when or the way we want them. Because God knows what we *need,* despite our insistence upon having what it is we *want*. Being a man is about checking your ego at the door, **setting pride aside**. Remembering what Phil 4:13 tells us – that it is through Christ, and not our own efforts, that we can do all things. It's about giving Him the glory in both victory and defeat. You can tell more about a man in defeat than victory. Never forget that people will watch to see how you handle loss, and that in loss you will have an opportunity to demonstrate true faith and character. A man is **never jealous**. A man is more focused upon what he has, as opposed to what he doesn't have. He considers what he has both a blessing and a responsibility. A man realizes that to whom much is given, much is expected. A man never sacrifices or compromises the gifts he has been given. A man maximizes these gifts to and for the benefit of others. He looks outward instead of inward, because he recognizes that it's not about him. A man is **not rude**. A man understands that from a woman's perspective, there is no greater compliment than to be called a gentleman - open doors, send flowers, be respectful, be polite, be kind. And smile. Realize and recognize that there is no such thing as anyone less or more important than you. Treat everyone you meet with the same dignity. Be **self-less**. A man sets aside his own desires and needs for others but also recognizes the importance of investing in himself so that there is more of him for others. A man learns from his past but doesn't stay there – he allows his experiences to refine him, but not define him. A man knows that God is in the recycling business and will use his pain for others gain. A man chooses his attitude. Daily. He recognizes that his attitude is a conscious choice, that he has an opportunity to impact others by being a light in what can often feel like a very dark world. A man **seeks the truth** in all things, and **speaks and acts when he sees injustice**. He understands that being a man is about responsibility and accountability. Both require *doing*. Finally, a man never ever gives up. He may give in when the situation requires, but he never gives up. He always **keeps the faith, perseveres**, and **endures** because he never forgets the promise of how it will all end.

Dare to Prepare

In October of 1911, two teams set out in a quest to become the first expedition to reach the South Pole. For one team, it would be a race to victory and a safe return home. For the second team, it would be a devastating defeat, reaching the pole only to find a wind-whipped flag of their rival planted 34 days earlier. All five members of that second team perished - from exhaustion, frostbite, and freezing to death as they wrote the very last words they would write to loved ones back home. Two teams, two different outcomes....both believed, but only one achieved. Why? Because simply believing is never enough. And yes, it's not lost on me that I'm the BELIEVE guy, but I can tell you from personal experience that believing is just the first step. While it's gotta be in place, you can't fly solo with it. In three weeks I run Boston. I believe I can run the 26.2 miles, but if I don't prepare (work my butt off), race day could be a miserable experience.

Norwegian Ronald Amundsen led the successful team's 1400 mile journey. He did it 20 miles a day, every day, with consistency regardless of the weather conditions. To prepare, he biked 2000 miles from Norway to Spain. He experimented with eating raw dolphin meat as a source to energy should he get shipwrecked en route. He spent time with Eskimos in advance to adopt their cold-weather survival techniques and see how they used dogs for sled pulling. He gathered 3 tons of food for 5 men. When asked why the depth of intentional preparation, Amundsen said

"You don't wait until you're in an unexpected storm to discover that you need more strength and endurance. You prepare with intensity, all the time, so that when conditions turn against you, you can draw from a deep reservoir of strength"

England's Robert Falcon Scott chose not to train his body in advance. He chose ponies over dogs to pull supplies, never having taken the time to study the Eskimos. He brought one ton of food for 17 men. He left no markings for his return back from the pole, which ultimately doomed him. Perhaps most importantly, he picked and chose which days his team would hike. When the weather was poor, they stayed in their tents. And consumed the food they eventually would run out of. The ponies proved a poor choice to pull supplies in the conditions they would face, and all would die before Scott's team succumbed to the elements and hunger. Scott's journal entries prior to his death typically said

"Our bad luck continues, another terrible day"

Believing is a must. But it's nothing without the will to prepare. Dues must be paid, sacrifices made. Anything worth achieving comes at a cost, and most of the preparation is the non-glamorous behind-the-scenes stuff that nobody really enjoys doing, but without which outcomes aren't possible. You can have all the faith in the world, but without the action, you'll be dead in the water. Or stranded at the South Pole. Are your preparing? Will you be ready? For in life, it's not matter of if, but *when*, a storm will hit.

Believe. Prepare. Achieve.

"In the same way, faith by itself, if it is not accompanied by action, is dead". -
James 2:17

On Love and Winter Running

There are few things in life more difficult than dragging one's butt out from under the warmth of a toasty down comforter, putting ten minutes worth of cold weather layered protection on, and then venturing out for a run directly into that dark, frigid, and often dangerous abyss which we call winter. In the spring the running is easy and simple. Maybe a t-shirt and shorts, typically bright sunshine and welcoming temps and always a smooth surface. But in winter running we endure the elements and make the daily, conscious choice to run in conditions that are never optimal. Some days it can be downright painful. One morning I awoke to find myself in weather 3 degrees above zero (Cedar Falls, Iowa) and realized a few minutes into my run that if I wanted to continue seeing out my eyes and stay focused on the road ahead I would need to thaw the ice from my eye lashes. I turned around and ran backwards for a stretch, allowing my back to bear the brunt of the wind while I bought myself some time thawing the ice which had crystallized around my eyes.

I don't necessarily *feel* like running through the winter but I do it, because I know that it's good for me. I know that the discipline of daily running, the consistency of choosing to push myself physically will pay dividends. I also know that if ever took the winter off and only ran when conditions were optimal or when I felt like it, I'd pay a huge price for my neglect. Trying to start back up when spring rolled around would prove difficult and no doubt painful.

The unconditional choice to run in the winter is similar to the unconditional nature regarding how we are called to love. Love is a choice, not a feeling. It is not a knee-jerk reaction, but rather an initiated action - much like the intentionality required to set an alarm clock, respond to that alarm, get the layers on, and get out the door. People will say that they have fallen "out of love", but effectively they've chosen to no longer love. They've not lost the feeling, they've simply decided to no longer *choose* to love that person. Much like running in the spring, loving when someone is lovable or when we deem them "deserving" of our love is easy. Choosing to love someone when they've wronged us or are not treating us with the respect or dignity we believe we deserve - well that's kinda like running in the winter. Rarely easy, often painful, but absolutely necessary if we are to live by the calling of the One who chooses to love *us* unconditionally.

I know this much. The spring *always* comes. And that's what keeps me running through the winter - sometimes it's just about holding on, getting through and enduring these dark months. Relationships are no different. If you hold on and love unconditionally even when you don't *feel* like it, there's a pay-off. As I have learned through running, the ability to push through the winter and persevere always strengthens my resolve and makes for far better runs by the time spring rolls around. **Believe.**

"Love bears all things, believes all things, hopes all things, _endures_ all things" -
1 Corinthians 13:7

Why I Still Believe

"Scattered words and empty thoughts, seem to pour from my heart
I've never felt so torn before, seems I don't know where to start
but it's now that I feel Your grace falls like rain,
from every fingertip, washing away my pain
I still believe in Your faithfulness. I still believe in Your truth.
I still believe in Your holy word.
Even when I don't see, I still believe." - Jeremy Camp

There are times in life when it's both easy and natural to doubt the existence of our God. When things happen which don't make sense, when the pain of an experience or a relationship is so deep and searing that it literally takes your breath away. When really bad things happy to really good people. When sin and evil seem to win out, even if for the moment. In these times, we search for meaning and come up wondering where God is in all of it and why He doesn't reach down, step in, and save the day. Why we must endure the suffering and tragic consequences of man's sinful nature.

It's really easy to believe when life is good, when we feel blessed, and when our lives are pain and trouble free. But I've also come to realize that during those times, it's also really easy to take our relationship with God for granted, to drift away and for space to come in between that relationship. How often do we go to God in prayer when it's all good? How often do we tend to believe that we remain both capable and in control when things are stable and smooth?

I don't believe God causes the pain and sponsors the sin in our lives, but I do believe He uses both for His greater purpose in our lives and in the lives of others. I have found that during those gut-wrenching and intensely painful times, when the hurt is overwhelming, I feel closest to Him. While I know He is always there, I also know that He desires a more personal and intimate relationship with me and quite often the only time I'm willing to slow down and move into a deeper relationship with Him is during my times of need. When I finally realize that I'm not in control, that I can't do it alone, when I can no longer make sense of what is playing out in my life. He doesn't want or cause the pain but He will use it to draw us closer to Him, in the hope that the relationship becomes both sustainable and unconditional - that we will someday come to *really* know Him and experience the depth of His love for us in ways which transcend the circumstances of our lives. When we finally give up the control and the idea that we can handle everything which comes our way.

I still believe, even when I don't *see* hope, reason, love, or purpose. I know it's there and I know each of these things will eventually be revealed if I simply continue to press forward in faith, never giving up or giving in. *BELIEVE.*

"Despite all these things, overwhelming victory is ours through Christ, who loved us. And I am convinced that nothing can ever separate us from God's love. Neither death nor life, neither angels nor demons, neither our fears for today nor our worries about tomorrow - not even the powers of hell can separate us from God's love. No power in the sky above or in the earth below - indeed, nothing in all creation will ever be able to separate us from the love of God that is revealed in Christ Jesus our Lord. - Romans 8: 37-39

Marathon Lessons for Life

I competed in Cincinnati's Flying Pig Marathon in the spring of 2011 and spent most of my 3+ hours out on the course in heavy rain thinking about the blog I was going to write after I survived the experience. It was my 35th marathon, but it was the only one I have ever done on a whim, signing up late Friday afternoon less than 48 hours before race time. I knew going in that the weather wasn't going to cooperate. I knew going in that my pre-race training wasn't good. I knew the course was advertised as "hilly". But I went through with it just the same and along the way did some thinking about life through the lens of a marathon.

1. **Conditions can make or break you - it's a matter of your perspective**: Pouring rain and rolling thunder greeted us as we stepped out of the cover of Paul Brown Stadium and up to the starting line. Remarkably, I didn't hear anyone complaining - people were reminding each other that "At least it isn't 80 degrees and sunny", "This rain will keep us cooled off","At least we won't dehydrate!". These folks knew there was literally nothing they could do about the rain - the only thing they could control was their attitude. Storms will roll through our lives but they will not stay - and staying positive in the midst of the storm and putting things in perspective will help ensure we get through whatever comes our way.

2. *Take things one mile at a time*: 26.2 miles is a long way to run. Standing on the starting line, it can be an overwhelming prospect to consider what's ahead. But when broken into smaller chunks, taken one mile at a time, it becomes more reasonable. I never allow myself to consider all of the miles before me - I take them as they come, one down, two down, three down... I set smaller goals within the race, deciding where I want to be at certain points along the way - I literally pick off the miles and the goals as I go along. Life's

challenges can feel like a tsunami at times, when taken on the whole. Break the challenges into chunks - daily victories, weekly mileposts, monthly gains. One by one, take something on and take it out. Move forward. Before you know it, you are on your way with miles behind you and the confidence that you will get to the finish line.

3. **In the midst of challenges, keep focused on the finish, and never lose faith**: Are you focused on the conditions (rain), the miles ahead, the challenges you encounter, or the amazing feeling of crossing that finish line? At mile 11, I noticed my insole/cushioned support riding up my ankle. My shoes were water-logged and the glue holding the insole had come off. I stopped, took my shoe off, fixed the insert, and carried on. A mile later, I'm feeling it happen again - so I strip my socks off hoping my bare feet would keep the insole in place. By mile 13, I'm losing the insole *again*, so I stop, take it out, and run without the cushioning and support . Each time, I made the adjustment and kept moving forward. I never lost hope, never despaired, never thought about packing it in. I just kept thinking about getting through to the finish - and I tried to banish any negative thoughts I had about my circumstances. I pressed on. Life's challenges can take us off track, if we allow them. But press on we must, despite what comes our way - even if those circumstances weren't of our choosing, we will be better for having persevered, for having kept the faith.

4. **Pace yourself**: Those who start out sprinting a marathon end up walking - and compromising their finish. I had hundreds of folks pass me early on, only to be passed during the last 10K. I hooked in with a 3:15 finish pace group from the start, and we kept a steady 7:30 (per mile) pace for every mile. I lost them when I had my shoe problems, but the steady, even pace helped ensure a strong finish. Life is a marathon - it's not a sprint. Pace is paramount - especially when up against challenges. Slow down, be deliberate, be intentional about your energy reserves always remembering that you are in it for the long haul.

5. **Surround yourself with encouragers**: I found fellow runners to lift up and to lift me up. I ran by a guy wearing the Phil 4:13 verse on the back of his shirt - he was walking, with six miles to go. I pulled up alongside him and said *"What part of "I can do ALL things through Christ who gives me strength" don't you believe right now?"* He thanked me for the reminder and started running again, toward the finish line. I found myself in no man's land (running solo) for awhile - no place you want to be - until the 3:20 pace group caught up with me. I was encouraged by the pace coaches who kept us all focused on the "one mile at a time" mantra, and I realized my mile splits were getting faster again. One coach kept telling us how strong we looked, (despite how we felt)....it was just what we needed, when we needed it. When life gets difficult, find folks who love you unconditionally, provide the support and encouragement you need when you need it, and help carry you through life's darkest moments.

6. **What doesn't kill me really does make me stronger**: Finish a marathon, and you realize there aren't too many things that come your way in this life that you can't get through. The process is painful, and there is always a price to be paid. But the tougher the circumstances, the tougher you come out the other side - refined by your struggles, case hardened, as they say. If you stay the course and overcome life's challenges - no matter how difficult - you will be better prepared for whatever comes your way down the road. Some of the strongest, most determined people I have met in life are those who have overcome and persevered through the most difficult personal circumstances.

7. **The tough times don't last forever - and the finish line is SO worth it**!: The hills may be brutal but they are temporary. The rain may be pelting your face but it stops. The course may seem like it's endless, but soon you see mile marker 26 and hear the crowds at the finish line less than a quarter mile away. Every ache and pain you felt just a few minutes ago now seems to have left you - a smile

returns to your face and no matter how many times you have done it before, it's an incredibly emotional moment. You think back to every sacrifice you made getting here, every challenge you overcame, every negative influence or relationship in your life you needed to rise above and move beyond. You have persevered, you have kept the faith through it all. The finish is your reward, and nobody can take it from you.

"I have fought the good fight. I have finished the race. I have kept the Faith" -

2 Timothy 4:7

Digging Deep

"But He said to me, My grace is sufficient for you, for my power is made perfect in weakness" - 2 Corinthians 12:9

The last few miles of a marathon or Ironman typically require you to go places both mentally and physically you'd rather not go; you feel completely tapped, the finish line seems to get further and further away despite your steps forward, and your pace often slows to a crawl. Even with the best preparation and pre-race planning, the last bit of any long distance race can be downright brutal. Those who have been there will tell you that there is another place they go, somewhere deeper into the soul to find both the physical and mental reserves required to get them through to the end. It's often during those moments of complete weakness that athletes find strength they never thought existed. The conversations with God usually re-start during those times as well...."God, just get me through these last few miles". When we are feeling our best, our strongest, our most confident, few of us actually think about God and fewer among us actually go to and rely upon Him. Like early on in a race, when we're feeling good and in the flow, full of energy and more than enough in the tank. He's there on call, in reserve, for those moments of doom, gloom, and despair when we can't see our way around a problem or out of a situation. It's not that He'd prefer it that way - He actually wants a relationship with us in all times, good and bad, victory and defeat, joy and pain. But He knows that His presence is often revealed and felt the most during our times of despair, His power made perfect in our weakness. It's during those times that we recognize and come to terms with the fact that we simply can't make it on our own, that He is in control, and that without Him we don't cross that finish line. Digging deep we find that it's not our own strength or reserves which get us through another day, but His power and might and that there is absolutely nothing that He can't take on. Digging deeper we find that He is in control, that He never leaves or forsakes us, that He allows for our moments of weakness and pain so that we might finally and fully experience His strength and healing presence. Don't despair. *BELIEVE.*

Unencumbered

Unencumbered: *Loaded to excess or **impeded** by a heavy load*

My summer runs are always my fastest - primarily because I'm not wearing much, save for a pair of light shorts. When I lived in Chicago, my winter runs were laboriously slow - not because I trained fewer hours or with less effort, but because I was so loaded up with layers of clothing to keep the cold, wind, snow, ice, sleet, etc. at bay. At times it was comical, I'm sure to passing motorists I looked like the Michelin Man. All of those extra clothes and that added weight simply bogs you down. And slows you down. You can't open it up and lengthen your stride because the layers constrict and restrict movement. It doesn't mean you can't get out and run, it's just that the quality of the run and your level of enjoyment can be hugely compromised. When summer rolls around and I can shed all of those extra layers, my movement becomes more natural, less encumbered, and running is pure joy again. I'm generally a bit lighter (weight-wise) come summer, usually ten pounds down as I'm just more active as I enjoy time outdoors. Less weight to carry = faster, smoother runs.

Winter layering, running encumbered, is a necessity - it protects us from the elements. One could choose to run only in shorts, but you'd do so at your own peril. As we go through this life, what we layer on and encumber ourselves with is a *choice*. Resentment, anger, intolerance, hatred, jealousy, disappointment, failure, rejection.....layer upon layer upon layer. All serving to burden our journey, **impeding** our progress, encumbering our walk and robbing us of any future joy that the Lord may have in store for our lives. The weight of those feelings can be crushing - we mistakenly think that harboring evil thoughts and ill will towards those who offend us serve to hurt the offender, but all too often those are the folks sleeping through the night while we toss and turn. Here's some simple advice - let it go. Peel away the layers, one by one, and start moving forward completely unencumbered. The journey is a lot more enjoyable, and life's effort is so much easier when you drop the extra baggage.

"Get rid of all bitterness, rage and anger, brawling and slander, along with every form of malice. Be kind and compassionate to one another, forgiving each other, just as in Christ God forgave you. " Ephesians 4:31-32

Loncoy's Legacy

I wrote the below as a tribute to a young man who attended my church, his name was Andrew Loncoy. As I was not blogging back when he passed away, the below was never published but it was shared with Andrew's family. I wanted to ensure his legacy from my perspective, made it into print.

I will always remember the first time I met "Longcoy", as the kids at A.C. Reynolds High School called him. I was at my daughter Emily's Cross Country meet one fall afternoon, it was at an away location, and he was seated in the driver's seat of the school bus the kids had taken to get there. He was a senior, and he had aspirations of becoming a school bus driver one day. Aspirations is perhaps the wrong word - he was a bit obsessed with the idea. He always had a smile on his face and a story to tell, if you let him. He loved buses and cars. He knew everything about them, or so it seemed. He reminded me a bit of the energizer bunny, he never stopped moving, laughing or talking. I recall that he didn't seem to care what others thought of how he acted, how he dressed, or how he talked. He was a bit slow, in terms of mental capacity, but that didn't stop him from being part of the social fabric of the high school. After he felt comfortable around me (and that didn't take too long!), referring to me as "Emily's Dad", he remarked how much he admired my VW Passat. He said VW's were his favorite cars.

The last time I saw Longcoy was in church. He was in his favorite front row seat, singing and dancing with arms lifted high as we sang the praise and worship song "He Reigns". I remember thinking about how cool he looked up there, freely expressing his love for his Lord, not thinking for a moment about what others thought of him and how he looked. I remember wanting to do the same, with the same reckless abandon, but clearly (if I was honest with myself) worried about what others would think of me - especially my kids, I didn't want to embarrass my kids! I chose to sing and watch Longcoy, admiring his every move and the innocence of his heart. The amazing thing about that experience was the irony of it all for me - I had developed an admiration for his natural, unabashed expression of his faith and he had developed an admiration for my car. It confirmed to me once again that my example to others needed to be greater than what I owned, who I knew, how I dressed, or how I "looked".

My daughter Emily called me from a sleepover at a friend's house late one Sunday night, awakening me at midnight to tell me that Andrew Clifford Longcoy hadn't made it home from our Church Picnic that day. He died tragically in a one-car accident, losing control of his car and hitting a tree. We talked for a bit, and I remember not having the right words to tell her. I thought about Longcoy's short, but full life all day that Monday, and that night around the dinner table we talked about the kid who longed to be a bus driver. Emily commented that for sure, he's in heaven, and God has him behind the wheel of a school bus.

I felt compelled to share Longcoy's brief story and his impact on my life. Next time I am in church, I will try to summon the courage and display the outward expression of love for his Creator which he showed week in and week out from the front row of Covenant Community Church.

Playing it Safe

While I enjoy running the trails and roads of Asheville, nothing beats running somewhere I haven't been, the opportunity to explore a new city first thing in the morning before the place comes to life. Most hotels now have running maps; safe, simple, typically short routes around the hotel or within just a mile or two of the grounds. I never ask for them. I throw caution to the wind and take off, sometimes after simply asking the bellman which direction I should head to best explore the area. In July of 2010 I visited Alaska for the first time – Anchorage, Fairbanks, and Juneau. In Anchorage, I ran downtown, eventually finding a trail which weaved its way along a beautiful, raging river filled with salmon. In Fairbanks, I followed an old gold mining road a few miles out and saw several moose and one lone white wolf. In Juneau, I ran from the airport hotel towards the seaport, along the way witnessing bald eagles diving down to steal fish from an estuary at low tide.

Here's my point. With every run, I had an option. Play it safe, stay close to the hotel running several short loops around the block or down the main drag and back. I'd get my run in just the same, gaining cardiovascular benefits and burning the same number of (beer) calories I consumed the night prior. It would have been boring as hell, but I could have checked the box in my Franklin Planner delivering another mini-endorphin kick that I get from accomplishing something. But here's what I would have missed; the moose, the wolf, the salmon, the bald eagles, the beauty and splendor of God's amazing creation that is unique to Alaska. It's the same option and decision no matter where I travel.

Our lives are filled with similar options and decision points. We feel safe in a job which we also feel lukewarm about doing. We'd much rather be pursuing something else God has called us to do, but we have a bills to pay and kids to feed and other people's expectations to meet. So we stick to the safe route, waking up every day and driving to work only to return nine hours later the same path home. The scenery doesn't change, but hey, it's comfortable and it's a job. Do you ever wonder what you might be missing out on? What if God has bigger plans, bigger visions, and an even more dramatic change in scenery in store? How long are you willing to play it safe, only ever experiencing a small slice of what could be? What is it that you're waiting on? It doesn't have to be your job – it could be an interest, passion or goal you've put off, going back to school to finish a degree, or a relationship you've been reluctant to pursue. God intends for us to explore life, with vigor and passion, living each day intentionally for Him, fulfilling the purpose which He has planned for our lives. Playing it safe gets us through to the end, but along the way we'll have missed out on all that we could have become or experienced.

"You were born an original. Don't die a copy." - John Mason

Holding On

"Hold on, baby hold on, 'cause it's closer than you think, and you're standing on the brink, hold on, baby hold, on 'cause there's something on the way, your tomorrow's not the same as today"

- **Kansas**

When I compete, there comes a time towards the end of the race when I'm feeling like I have nothing left to give. I've put out the effort and energy and I'm really feeling it; the pain can be pretty intense. I try to reach deeper into the tank for that final stretch run to the finish, but there's not much left. It's decision time - whether or not I finish generally isn't in question, but HOW I finish remains in doubt. So many thoughts run through my head.....how much longer can I hold on, how much more pain can I endure, why does every body part hurt, why did I sign up for this @$@*# race, why does this have to be so hard? Holding on and pushing through the pain and doubt in the midst of a competition's most difficult moments is not easy - but it's necessary. I *always* find that by getting through these moments and persevering through to the finish, giving more than I thought I had in me, I come out stronger and more capable.

For me, these tough race moments mirror life's most challenging times. How do you hold on for one more day when you feel like you've given all? How can you get through what seems impossible? You simply decide that these moments will not get the best of you, that there will be a tomorrow and you will be there to see it. Holding on requires that you surround yourself with people who love you, care for you, and will encourage you. Holding on requires taking the focus off yourself and investing in the needs of others - you'll find there is always someone hurting more than you. Holding on requires taking specific actions which will serve to strengthen and sustain you for the long run. And holding on requires taking all of your anxieties and concerns to the One who cares for you (1 Peter 5:7).

Anyone can give up, it's the easiest thing in the world to do. But to hold on when everyone else would understand if you packed it in, that's true strength."

So hold on. Don't give in. Keep the Faith. Endure....and **BELIEVE!**

"He conquers who endures." ~Persius

Running on Faith

One of the beautiful things about a marathon is that it is SO long that you simply can't focus on your race effort for the entire 26.2 miles. One of the toughest things about a marathon is that it is SO long that you simply can't focus on your race effort for the entire 26.2 miles. What makes the race both incredible and challenging is that there is so much time for your mind to wander, so many opportunities for reflection and for self-doubt to creep in, so many times you can go back and forth between belief and fear. Regardless of how well you have prepared physically, anyone who has finished a marathon knows that at some point it's hugely mental. Come in with the wrong focus and it's going to be a long day. While I was well prepared physically for the 114th running of the Boston Marathon in 2010, I was far from mentally focused. Sometimes life gets in the way of plans we make well in advance, and it's during those times that God chooses to use our circumstances to make a point. So often in life we think that we can go it alone, following our own agenda and running on our own strength and will. Just when we think we've got everything under control, the rug comes out from under us and we're forced to recognize that ultimately, we are not in control. I knew going into Boston that there was no way I'd run my best without turning my race over to Him. The course is just too tough - especially over the second half. The first 13 miles are basically flat to downhill, but from 13 through 21 your climbing through the hills of Newton culminating in the famous "Heartbreak Hill". Once over the top, it's downhill again into Boston, past Fenway Park, and through to the finish on Boylston. The ups and downs show no mercy on your legs, turning them to Jell-O somewhere between miles 22 and 23. It was all pretty daunting, despite my preparation. In the days leading up to the race, I was intentional about taking my doubts to Him in prayer - asking for the focus and strength to persevere so that my effort might reflect His amazing power and love. The day of the race

I posted Isaiah 40:31 on my Facebook status....

"but those who hope in the LORD will renew their strength. They will soar on wings like eagles; they will run and not grow weary, they will walk and not be faint."

I had officially turned it all over to Him. For the first time in many weeks, I had this calm about me - a peace that passes all understanding. I was ready, knowing that my effort would not be my own. As the race unfolded, I found renewed strength and focus. And for the first time in 13 years doing Boston, I actually ran a negative split! In non-runner terminology, that means I covered the second 13.1 faster than the first half. It means that somehow I went faster up the hills than down. I found myself passing people up and over Heartbreak. I was encouraged by the crowd, many people responding to my TEAM 4:13 race shirt. And as I took that last turn onto Boylston with the finish line in sight some 400 yards away, knowing that I had just covered the course faster than any I had covered in seven years, the emotions let loose and I looked and pointed skyward....I had persevered, running on Faith, for His glory - an example that I hope resonates with others. **I BELIEVED**!

"Blessed is the man who perseveres under trial, because when he has stood the test, he will receive the crown of life that God has promised to those who love him. " - James 1:12

When It's Time to Let Others Pull

Any cyclist knows that when you get dropped off the back of a group ride and you lose the pack, your ride becomes significantly more difficult - especially when you are riding into a headwind. There's a reason people ride in packs (and no, contrary to what most drivers believe, it is not to irritate those trying to get somewhere in a hurry). There is absolutely NO WAY you can maintain the same speed/pace/effort. It's called a draft, and the same holds true but to a lesser extent in open water swimming and long distance running. When people take turns "pulling" and then tucking back in after they have spent some time cutting the wind for everyone else, the efficiency of the entire group can improve by as much as 30% vs. everyone going solo expending individual effort against the headwinds. Because of the recognized advantage gained by drafting, most Triathlons do not allow folks to draft - do it more than once and you get DQ'd.

We were never designed by God to face life headwinds on our own. When people struggle with difficult situations and challenging circumstances, and they doubt God's presence in their lives at that time, it's most likely because they have chosen to go through it alone. Going solo into the eye of a storm is a recipe for disaster. God has surrounded us with people who love us, care about us, believe in us, and truly want the best for us. I believe that casting your burdens on Him also involves being vulnerable, transparent, and open with friends and family so that much like in a group ride, they can surround us, cut some of the headwind for us, and see us through to the finish line....Acts 14:22 reminds us,

"Where they helped the believers to grow in love for God and each other. They encouraged them to continue in the faith in spite of all the persecution, reminding them that they must enter into the Kingdom of God through many tribulations"

While our faith may be strong, there are those times in life when our faith may not be enough to carry us through - but combined with the faith, love, and support of friends and family, our faith becomes stronger, able to withstand that which we once thought impossible to face. So know when to let others pull.....drop back and behind your friends, and let them help carry you with God's strength through to the other side. BELIEVE!

The Greater the Battle, the Greater the Victory

If there's one thing I've learned over the past few years, it's that everyone is fighting something. Nobody has the "perfect" life. Looks can be deceiving....some people appear to be holding up, doing well, getting by, but deep inside they are hurting. They're dealing with financial stress, marital discord, issues with their kids, their elderly parents, or problems at work. If you ask those who are hurting what they are praying for, they'll tell you they'd really like God to take away the problem - remove the pain, return things to the way they were. But 2 Corinthians 12:9 reminds us, that God's "grace is sufficient for you, His strength is made perfect in weakness". In "*Breaking Intimidation*", John Bevere writes of Paul's struggles with accepting the persecution he encountered while preaching the Gospel. On numerous occasions, Paul pleaded for the Lord to take away the pain and suffering which came his way, but God essentially says

"Paul, don't ask Me to remove these things, but rather ask that My grace and strength will raise you above what you cannot handle. Where there are no obstacles, there is no need for power. A victory can occur only where there is a battle. The greater the battle, the greater the victory! A true soldier does not run from conflict, but runs to it. In the heat of the battle is not the time to ask God to take us out of the war. It is the time to pray for His grace so that we may TRIUMPH in it. God is glorified when we face something impossible to overcome in our humanness. It is then that His strength rests on us for all to see."

And so it is....as difficult as the battle often seems, we need to proceed in faith and recognize that He is at work. The last few miles of an Ironman are never pretty. You've battled all day long, you don't think you've got anything left to give, but you dig deep and push through to the finish. On your own, it may not have been possible - and on your own, you may have opted to quit, to be taken out of the battle. But with and through Him, you come to know that anything is possible and that He is glorified through the effort. And you just know, that every step of the way, He had you right where He wanted you - relying not on your own strength and endurance, but upon His......*BELIEVE!*

Relax, It's His Move

Somedays I wake up way too early....the wrong side of 4 AM....and my mind is racing. I'm wondering about my next move, what the future will hold, how I will deal with those issues which seem so overwhelming. I have that pit in my stomach that won't go away. My life has been pretty much stress free, but God has a way of getting your attention sometimes and it often doesn't feel very good. So I reach for a book I have read by Mark Batterson, "**In a Pit with a Lion on a Snowy Day**", and I find words which provide comfort and settle the storm within. Mark writes,

"Think of your life as a game of chess. You are the pawn and God is the Grand Master. You have no idea what your next move should be, but God already has the next 200 million moves planned out. Some of His moves won't make sense, but that is simply because we can't compute 200 million contingencies at a time! We've just got to trust the Grand Master. God wants you to get where God wants you to go more than you want to get where God wants you to go. Now here's the catch: Sometimes His itinerary entails coming face to face with a lion in a pit on a snowy day (read the story of Benaiah, from 2 Samuel). Not a good place to be. But when you find yourself in those challenging circumstances, you need to know that God is ordering your footsteps. You can have a sense of destiny because you know that God has considered **EVERY** *contingency in your life, and He* **always** *has your best interest at heart. And that sense of destiny, rooted in the sovereignty of God, helps you pray the unthinkable and attempt the impossible".*

In the words of the Psalmist, "I look behind me and you're there, then up ahead and you're there too". How comforting is that? So all of the worry, all of the stress, all of the consternation - why do we carry it? It actually suggests a lack of faith. Trust me, I know it's not easy to internalize. But I always tell people to "**Keep the Faith**", now it's time for me to take my own, good, godly advice. **BELIEVE.**

Does it Define or Refine you?

Setbacks are part of life. I've had my share...and guess what? I now come to expect them. Not that I'm ever thrilled (initially) that they are upon me, but I've learned that they can be good things. At a point in my life, I allowed them to define me - who I was, what I was worth, what other people thought of me. I assumed that professional setbacks were some kind of sign that I wasn't capable, or good enough at doing whatever it was I was doing. I assumed that personal setbacks were roadblocks put up to prevent me from realizing my dreams. In each and every case, both personally and professionally, the setbacks were temporary and they eventually led me to pursue paths which helped me realize dreams (personally) and pursue passions (professionally). So now when someone tells me that I'm not going to be getting that role that I thought I "deserved", I get over my disappointment pretty quickly and then seek God's guidance - "OK, where is it that you need me, if not here?". When I get injured during training right before a big race, I accept my plight and assess my alternatives - "OK, this isn't turning out the way that I had planned, but show me Your plan and how can I glorify You through what has happened to me!". You can either let setbacks define you or *REFINE* you.... "**to improve or to perfect you**". At the time, whatever it is you are going through doesn't feel like it's serving to improve or perfect you, but ultimately it does and it will, provided you Keep the Faith - and seek the answer to the question, "What is it that I'm supposed to learn from this?" In the end, the sense of accomplishment and joy which comes from realizing that dream or pursuing that passion will feel that much more amazing and taste that much sweeter because of the setbacks you experienced - and overcame - along the way. Stop the defining and embrace the **REFINING!**

BELIEVE. PHIL 4:13

There is Purpose in the Pain

Many of my blogs involve a running story - in large part, because running is a passion of mine, but also because long runs tend to provide me with some great alone time where my thoughts drift and then come together to form concepts I otherwise wouldn't have taken the time to think through. This morning was no different....I headed out in the dark, 22 degree temps, with a biting wind and icy roads to greet me. As I'm shuffling (carefully) down my steep neighborhood hill and out onto Rt. 74, only a few minutes into the run, I kept thinking "Wouldn't it be great if I could just fast-forward to the end of this run, when I'd be pulling back into my driveway and the comfort and warmth of my home?" I could avoid the cold, the wind, the searing burn in my lungs as I crested the last big hill. I could avoid the pain, aches, and fatigue which often accompany my longer runs. If it were just that easy....over before it started, yet achieving the same benefits! Fully prepared for the Boston Marathon in April without the tests along the way. And then I thought about the current personal challenges I'm facing. I emailed my dad the other day and shared with him that I just wish sometimes that I could fast-forward through these very painful, dark, uncertain times and get to the other side - where happiness, stability, and blue skies await. He reminded me that pain and suffering are part of life, that all of it serves a purpose which we can't see right now, but if we remain faithful and know that God will never desert us, He will bring us through all circumstances. And once we come out the other side, we'll be stronger, more faithful people better prepared for future challenges and more Christ-like in our character. Those who are never tested rarely get to *know* what faith is all about, and when that big test finally hits them, they are ill-prepared and often break. Without the 12 weeks of long run tests which build my endurance and my body's ability to handle the pain and fatigue, there would be no way I'd survive the 26.2 miles from Hopkinton to Boston. So I stay focused and trust God through all trials, knowing that He knows the outcome and believing His promise to never forsake me. There is a finish line for every race, and when you arrive, the pain, suffering, and fatigue subsides and you bask in the glory, His glory - not just of the finish, but of the journey that prepared you for the test.

1 Peter 5:10

"And after you have suffered a little while, the God of all grace, who has called you to his eternal glory in Christ, will himself restore, confirm, strengthen, and establish you."

BELIEVE!

Finding Yourself Back Where You Started

(Written April 14, 2013 – The day before the Boston Marathon Bombings.)

Tomorrow I run Boston. Anyone who has run it knows the course well. It's a straight route north from Hopkinton to Ashland through Wellesley up the hills of Natick down into Brookline and finishing on Boylston Street in downtown Boston. Not only has the course remained the same, but there are thousands of people running it with me and millions of people lining the race route and race officials, police, EMT, and volunteers there to be sure you know where you're going. There's no guessing. I can put all of my effort and energy into running the race and getting to the finish line. I have run races where the course isn't mapped or marked well - trust me when I say that there is nothing more frustrating in a race than getting lost and finding yourself back at the same point where you got lost, energy expended but not one step closer to the finish.

Dr. Jan Souman of the Max Planck Institute for Biological Cybernetics has actually studied what humans do when we have no road map, no clue about where we're going...simply put, when we're lost. He's researched what happens to folks when they find themselves in the woods, out to sea, or in the desert without a compass or navigation tools. His findings? We go in circles. Literally. Our instincts fail us. Without a guiding light or a True North to follow, we keep ending up at the starting point where we got lost. All of the effort and energy we put in is literally wasted. Even if you have never been lost, you inherently know that effort and energy are finite resources - they eventually run out.

Do you have a course map for your life? Do you have a Way, or do you find yourself ending up in the same place you started, having wasted valuable effort and energy only to have repeated the same failures and disappointments, still feeling incredibly lost and empty? Our time here on this earth is finite. Time lost going in circles is time we won't get back. The clock keeps running. When you know where you're going, when you have direction and guidance and a clear vision of where it is you're headed, none of the effort and energy you expend is wasted. Every step is a step forward, a step closer to the finish. I'm not saying it'll be easy. Just as I will experience tomorrow, while the course map remains established and known, I will still feel pain and experience suffering. But I can rest in the assurance that even the difficult, painful steps along the way are serving a purpose of getting me that much closer to the finish. And oh what a finish it will be! *Believe*.

John 14:6 "*And Jesus answered, I am the Way, the Truth, and the Life*"

Staying Focused on the Light

One chilly November morning, it was beyond dark when I pulled my car into Gettysburg College's fitness center and headed out for my run through the battlefields. Adding to the darkness was the cold; a raw chill mist rose from the grounds as I made my way from the lighted parking lot out into the National Park. I love running the access roads which weave throughout the fields, but the downside at that hour during an overcast morning is that you can't see a thing. Well, you can't see *most* things.....there is an eternal light peace memorial which sits atop Oak Hill and it's visible from 20 miles away. So when I run that early, I keep my focus on that eternal light - I head towards it, and as I get closer it's amazing how much better I can see things around me. It's also no coincidence that my pace quickens - I'm much more efficient and running just seems easier when I can see where I'm going. If I ever take my focus off the light, I soon find that I am off the road and in a field somewhere further away from my intended destination. Usually by the time I get to the light, the horizon is welcoming the first glimpse of the sun and the rest of my run is in the light. The difference, as they say, is night and day.

You would think that after 30+ years of running, I'd have learned that running safely through the darkness requires either bringing your own light or staying focused on one (like the peace memorial). You would also think that someone who writes a faith-based fitness blog would take his own good advice and always stay in the Light or follow the Light in his personal life. But just as I lose focus during my runs, taking my eyes off the light which safely guides my path through the battlefields, I lose focus in life and drift off the road and into *life's* battlefields - where land mines await, and hope is quickly extinguished in the darkness. The important point I'm making here is that I'm the one who has taken my eyes and my focus off His light. In John 8:12, Jesus tells us *"I am the Light of the world. Whoever follows me will never walk in darkness, but will have eternal life.*" He's always there, just like the eternal light peace memorial. It's a 24/7, 365 day thing. His light never goes out either. And while we WILL encounter darkness in our lives, there will always be His light to guide us back, to bring us home, and to show us the way through and out of the darkness, provided we stay focused on Him and never lose hope. **BELIEVE.**

When You Find the Way, It Changes Your Why

In February of 2013 I was in the middle of training for my 15th Boston Marathon, and after all of the years at it, I can say that I still enjoy the process. It's not the race itself so much - I know the course like the back of my hand, I get that *"been there, done that"* feeling when I'm standing at the starting line, and it's still an incredibly painful proposition especially as I advance in age :) to push myself 26.2 miles up and down the hills of greater Boston across the finish line on Boylston. What I enjoy most is the journey, the three-month build up as I put in the long training runs and drop the weight, the daily routine of rising out of bed and lacing up the running shoes with Purpose and the Vision of crossing that finish line on April 15th. You see, when I've got a race like Boston out in front of me, it changes who I am, what I'm doing, and why I'm doing it. Having a "Why" gets you out of bed in the morning. It's far harder to stay under the warmth of my down comforter on a cold, dark morning when you have a Why like Boston. Why get up and get out? Because I want to be my best on race morning. I want to know in my heart that I've done everything possible to prepare, no excuses, no regrets, no compromise. I know as well that God has gifted me with the physical talent and the mental tenacity to run, and run well - and I will not sacrifice that gift. Each morning I arise with a smile on my face and joy in my heart knowing that I *get* to do this. Running Boston is an honor, something many can only dream about doing.

When you come to know the Lord and have a personal relationship with Him, it changes your Why in much the same way. You wake up each day with greater clarity of Purpose and a Vision of the end game, the ultimate finish line. When I came to Christ, it literally changed who I was and how I conducted myself each day. My priorities changed, much like adding the discipline of running miles and miles as I prepare for a marathon, I began intentionally spending time in the Word and trying to be His light to a world in need of His message of hope, love, acceptance, and grace. As with the preparation for an impending marathon, I began to look at my time and the hours in the day in a much different way. My attitude and outlook on life changed dramatically as I began to see who I could be - not for me, but for others. Truthfully, from that day forward, I no longer needed an alarm clock to get up each day. I awake with passion, energy, and enthusiasm for everything that God would have in store for me as the day unfolds. I look forward to the journey now, even more so than the finish line. I enjoy the process of personal refinement and I know that He is preparing me for the race set before me, a race far more important than the prestigious Boston Marathon. *BELIEVE.*

"Therefore, since we are surrounded by such a huge crowd of witnesses to the life of faith, let us strip off every weight that slows us down, especially the sin that so easily trips us up. And let us run with endurance the race God has set before us." -Hebrews 12:1

What You Don't Know CAN Hurt You

When I was growing up, my parents were full of idioms they felt compelled to share with me as points of learning. Two I remember repeated often were "Ignorance is bliss" and "What you don't know won't hurt you". They seemed to go hand in hand, and when mentioned enough times I became convinced that there were things in life which I was better off not knowing. I bought the concept at the time but as I grew older and wiser, I came to see the flaw in the supposed logic.

While competing for Team USA and getting ready for the World Triathlon Championships off the Gold Coast in Australia in 2011, I did most of my pre-race swim training in the channel adjacent to my hotel. It was always clear of boats and there was never another swimmer to worry about. I had the water to myself. After a few days of mile swims back and forth across the inlet, I was finishing up my last swim and heard some local Australian yelling at me from the bridge above. He called me out of the water and waved me up to where he was, right next to a sign that I obviously hadn't seen from my entry point beach-side each day "WARNING: DO NOT swim in this channel, it is full of Bull Sharks!"

I went back to my room and became less ignorant about bull sharks. Here's what I learned - they are the world's most likely shark to attack humans. They favor shallow, coastal waters, which is also, not coincidentally, where people swim. They average 7-11 feet long, far smaller than their Great White cousins but more prone to travel in and attack in packs. They love to rip and shred those things with which they come into contact. Nice :)

The obvious lesson for me was to have been better informed.

Ignorance could have been deadly. What I didn't know could have killed me. Literally. It goes without saying that I steered very clear of those waters from that day forward. Not knowing something or lacking an awareness can seem momentarily blissful, but life is filled with things that we must come to know if we are to minimize pain, suffering, or in the worst case, a premature death. The signs are often everywhere, but in our blissful and ignorant nature, we often miss them. As a Believer, I've come to know that the One who created me put all of the warnings and instruction in one place for me to read. And He did so out of *LOVE*. Knowing this now, the choice remains mine. I can remain ignorant and temporarily blissful by ignoring His word and wisdom, or I can strive to gain and apply His knowledge to my walk in this world. It's not a guarantee that I'll avoid all of life's problems, but it will, no doubt, keep those problems I would have created on my own to the absolute minimum. And it will surely keep me out of the life's shark-infested waters. *BELIEVE*.

"My son, give attention to my words; incline your ear to my sayings. Do not let them depart from your sight; keep the in the midst of your heart. For they are life to those who find them, and health to all their whole body" - Proverbs 4:20-22

Destination Known

It's called the Spartan Ultra Beast, and it was the single most difficult physical challenge I have ever endured. I say endured because it was roughly 30 miles up and down Killington Mt, with 52 different obstacles along the way each one designed by a sadistic race director determined to ensure that less than 50% of the 386 athletes selected from thousands of applicants actually found the finish line. Everything about the race was a mystery, save for the start/finish line. I literally had no idea what I was getting myself into when I applied, as the race organizers made it abundantly clear that this event was about the "unknown" and we were to fear that which we did not know. It was the first of it's kind in the history of endurance sports which helped Team Spartan build and hype the fear factor - nobody had ever done it and only a short list of people associated with the event knew what awaited us when the gun went off.

At the starting line, I had a sense of peace despite the fact that I had no clue how the miles would unfold or how much physical torture lay ahead. I looked around and saw fellow competitors nervously preparing Camelbak's, Powerbars, and salt tablets and I got the sense even the most tested and hardened athletes knew that they couldn't have properly prepared for a race about which they knew nothing. But here's what I *did* know and what I focused upon....the finish line. I knew, regardless of how nasty, ugly, difficult, relentless, uncomfortable, and painful the course and the day would be, it would eventually end. The terrain and the obstacles were indeed unknown, but I knew what the finish line looked like and I knew that if I kept my focus on the finish - despite what I encountered along the way - I'd persevere. I also knew how incredibly amazing it would feel to finish, to be one of the 162 competitors receiving the coveted Ultra Beast medal. It turned out to be 11 hours and 36 minutes of sheer brutality, the unknown slowly became known as the race moved along (at a 27 minute per mile pace for me!), and I did finish under the cover of darkness in a driving rainstorm with temperatures falling into the upper 40's. I was bloodied, bruised, battered, but not broken. I had endured the day because I had not dwelt upon the unknown, keeping my focus instead upon the known.

Each day we face the unknown as the course of our lives unfolds before us. You've heard the phrase "Nobody knows what tomorrow may bring" and it's true. Sometimes life is brutal. Very often, it sucks. We are bloodied, bruised, and battered but we don't have to be broken by the challenges we face. What's known is how it will all end and Who will never leave us, regardless of how nasty, ugly, difficult, relentless, uncomfortable, and painful things get. Zephaniah 3:17 reminds us that "*The Lord our God is with us, always*" and John 3:16 lets us know what awaits, what *is* known *"For God so loved the world, that he gave his only Son, that whoever believes in Him should not perish but have <u>eternal life</u>*. This is how it ends for Believers.

So move forward in faith my friends, focusing on the finish, upon how overwhelmingly incredible and amazing it will feel to be Home with the One who never left or abandoned us along the way, regardless of the obstacles we encountered. **BELIEVE.**

Called to Encourage

I'll chalk it up to the fact that I am no techno-geek and it takes me far too long to figure out how to fully use all of the functionality designed into anything electronic. Way too early this morning I pulled myself out of bed and over to the stadium at Chambersburg High School for my weekly dose of speed (that would be mile repeats on a track). As my body semi-rejected any efforts to "warm-up" with a slow first mile, the powerfully transcendent beat of Pat Benatar's "Invincible" played through my I-Phone and into my ear buds to help kick-start the first mile. My schedule called for eight miles, each mile at a descending pace, with the plan to cover the last mile fastest. I felt great as the miles broke under my feet in the dark stadium, and soon the first signs of daylight slipped through the horizon and I had one mile left before packing it in. It goes without saying that the last one is the toughest, most painful mile of them all. To that point, the music had been perfect, marking my pace and encouraging my effort. Just as I was to start that last mile though, Pink Floyd's "Comfortably Numb" locked in on shuffle. To my earlier admission, NO, I do not yet know how to establish play lists. So the beat slows, and I wonder out loud how the heck I am going to dig deep and go harder for one last mile when a song so depressing and downbeat is playing? I could feel my pace slow and the effort that it now took to run as fast as I was previously running, let alone faster, seemed overwhelmingly daunting. What a difference a song makes! I finished out the workout but it was more of a struggle than it should have been.

When we hit difficult, challenging times in life what we need most is the encouragement and support of positive and caring friends - I've come to know that there are people in my life that I must surround myself with during tough times because they'll help get me through. Likewise, there are folks I need to avoid like the plague during life's darkest moments because they'll only serve to bring me down lower. As Christians we are called to encourage one another in our respective walks, we are called to uplift, support, embolden, and love. Everyone is carrying a burden of some kind. Everyone at some point is on that last, toughest mile of a problem and what they need from us is a little Pat Benatar. In 1 Thessalonians 5:11 Paul commands that we *"...encourage one another and build up one another, just as you also are doing."* God knew there would be "times like these" when we'd need a boost, a dose of positivity, an encouraging word, so that we could endure. Because sometimes life is simply about enduring. Who are *you* being for people? Who are you helping endure? **Believe** and Encourage, because you can't have one without the other.

On Feeling Worthy

It's been said that looks are deceiving. I was riding and running the battlefields of Gettysburg yesterday in the oppressive heat and humidity of South Central PA and while I probably looked OK on the outside I was suffering on the inside. The elements were taking a toll....there's something to be said for acclimation and clearly I was not yet acclimated to my new environment. I had become so used to the relatively cooler and less humid training conditions in the mountains of Asheville. I finished the workout and soon realized that I was pretty dehydrated, and my core body temperature was continuing to rise despite the fact that I had stopped training. It took a few hours and lots of water and Gatorade to get everything back to "normal".

Most people look OK on the outside but on the inside, they're suffering. They have, over time, become defined by their wounds, wounds which eventually make them become someone they're not. When I noticed what was happening on the inside yesterday, it was vital that I stopped to address my physical needs. Far too often we learn to adapt (emotionally) and accept the wounds as part of who we are and invariably we become a far lesser, reduced, and compromised version of whom God intended us to be. We feel less than worthy. We feel less than lovable. We sometimes lose that smile, that passion, that zest, and that capacity to love which once defined and drove us. We have allowed others to determine our worthiness, and we've somehow become convinced that we are undeserving of love and unconditional acceptance.

Emotional wounds are a reality of life. Nobody gets through unscathed. But remaining damaged and scathed is a conscious choice, carrying the constant reminders of what was done to us and allowing our history to rob us of a future filled with joy and possibility was never part of His plan for our lives. God reminds us in Isaiah 43:4 that we are "***precious in His sight, that we are honored and He loves us***" Knowing that, why would we continue to allow ourselves to be defined as less than worthy by anyone else? Why wouldn't we stop, assess the damages, and reconcile with our past so that the days ahead can be lived out loud with uncompromising passion and love? We belong to a God who not only believes we are worthy but loves us even when we are not lovable, and even with our imperfections. We are worthy. Believe. And then move forward in such a way that people come to see the Light again in you.

Hope in the Midst of it All

I always try to encourage people by telling them to keep the faith. A couple of years ago, it was just a saying, words that I uttered but didn't really understand or internalize. It was easy for me to say and do because I never *really* had anything which tested that faith. Sure, I hit some pretty low depths during endurance events, but those were more physical, temporary, and clearly self-induced. Now, having been through some of life's "worst" offerings and come out on the other side, I can share those words with the full knowledge that through it all, God's steadfast love never ceases and his mercies never fail us. Keeping the faith has new, deeper meaning. When faith is all you have to cling to, it's good to know that it is enough.

I recently re-connected with a high school buddy of mine while on business in the Boston area, and we met for a lunchtime run in Wellesley at the start of the toughest part of the Boston Marathon course. From the starting line in Hopkinton into Wellesley, it's basically 13.1 miles of rolling downhills. From Wellesley through Newton culminating with Heartbreak Hill, you have nearly 8 miles of uphill. We were catching up on nearly 30 years of life since graduation when the hills began to take their toll causing him to slow down and eventually walk. While he recovered his breath, our discussion turned to faith. *"I don't know what people do without faith,"* he stated. *"In some of my darkest moments I always knew there was hope, in the midst of it all, something to cling to."*

I hadn't given much thought to where we had met or why I had picked that location as our starting point, but in retrospect it served as a great reminder to us both of how much we had endured and yet become even more steadfast in our faith. The "hills" of life had served out their purposes, slowing us down but ultimately serving to strengthen our respective faiths, emboldened by the knowledge that we were both very different people than we had been while coasting through life's flat and otherwise downhill (read: easier) sections. Our common bond and renewed belief had, after all of these years, brought us together on this day to remind one another that God never brings us *to* something without bringing us *through* something. Our hope is in Him, the one who took the worst this world had to offer upon Himself, in the person of Jesus Christ, so that we can keep the faith and have hope even in the midst of life's most difficult days. *BELIEVE.*

"Yet I still dare to hope, when I remember this:
The faithful love of the LORD never ends! His mercies never
cease".

Where You Go

I came upon the father and son two miles into my run; the boy was no older than five, his dad just enough in front of him to lead the way as they navigated the Mountains to Sea trail on a beautiful Autumn day. Covered in a thick bed of fallen leaves, the path ahead wasn't always clear but I could tell the father knew where he was going and the son seemed to know he was in good hands. After hitting the turnaround point three miles into my 10K run, I'm returning back on that same path and the two hikers come into sight again, but this time the son is out just ahead of his dad - not too far but enough to make it seem like he was the one blazing the trail. I caught the boy looking back every few steps just to make sure his father was still there, and with every glance of confirmation I could see the boy picking up pace and gaining confidence that he was headed in the right direction. Just before our paths crossed for the second time I noticed that the boy had stopped, right in front of a large tree that had fallen across the trail. He patiently waited for his father to lift him up over it. As I passed them I wished them both a great walk and I finished out the last few miles of my run.

Over those miles I couldn't help but think about the relationship between that father and son, and the intentional approach the dad had with his young boy - how it parallels God's approach with us as we walk our life's journey. Sometimes He's out in front of us, guiding and leading our way as we navigate the path - He's never too far out ahead (it only feels that way when we forget to include Him in our thoughts and we are less than intentional with our prayer life). Other times He's right behind us, allowing us to pursue a path but available for counsel and guidance as our personal GPS should we ever doubt that the path is the right one. Either way, He is right there, as He promises in Matthew 28:20 "*I am with you always, even to the end of time.*"

We are all like that five-year old boy even as we grow, age, and experience life. We'll never reach that point where we can go it alone without the guidance of our Father. The trail ahead is far too difficult, filled with too many obstacles and challenges. We often try, but we soon realize we're lost, wandering aimlessly and often dangerously close to losing all the good that God has intended for us. The closer we remain to Him the less overwhelming those obstacles and challenges seem when we do encounter them; because it's not a matter of if, but when. And during those times, our Father picks us up, holds us closer, and carries us over and through the challenge. The obstacle isn't taken away, it's just endured. And when we are over it and on the other side, we can look back knowing that He was right there with us the whole time. **BELIEVE.**

The Daily Grind

I was five weeks out from the NYC Marathon and found myself needing to do a 22 mile long run as my second to last +20 miler in advance of the race. On the road attending Catalyst Leadership Conference just outside Atlanta, I knew getting in the run would require some sacrifice - with an 8:30 AM start, my wake-up call would be 4:30 AM with a run start of 5 AM to ensure completion by 8 AM which would mean early to bed as well. Needless to say, it's completely dark at that time, so a well-lighted loop would have to do. The night prior I mapped out a one mile course around a strip mall departing from my hotel.

I headed out into what still felt like night despite my Timex watch telling me otherwise. And so the loops began. To keep track of each one, I picked up small rocks and placed one on the curb near my Hampton Inn each time I passed by...there was nothing eventful or pretty about the run. The scenery rarely changed. Boring and routine would describe each pass by the front entrance to Kroger's grocery store, which marked about the half-way point for each lap. There were very few people and even fewer cars with which to contend, and after awhile I knew every curb, corner, and crack along the way. While I tried my best to stay in the moment, my focus was clearly on the finish - I did fight off the momentary lapses during which that logical part of my brain shouted "Bag this, pack it in, you've done enough and it's way too early in the morning anyway - it's simply not worth grinding this thing out". But grind it out I did, and coming around to finish that last mile proved sweeter than expected - I had prevailed and persevered over the boredom and routine, driven both by fanatical discipline and a desire to ensure I was ready for the event.

Preparing for a marathon is generally neither glamorous nor fun. It's hard work and it's routine. You carve out the time and make sacrifices along the way knowing the investment of effort will pay off on race day when you are rewarded for your commitment and dedication. Whenever I complete an endurance event, I look back on the several month journey which got me to the starting line, and I recognize this it was the process and the boring and uninspiring daily grind which made the joy of crossing the finish line possible. *Everything* that's worthwhile in life takes perseverance. Including relationships. Romance novels, Lifetime movies, and society in general often convince us that our lives are lacking excitement, that the grass is greener, and that there are people out there who will make us happier. But the myth is simply just that. Much of what we do together as couples constitutes the daily grind....paying bills, transporting kids to/from practices, cleaning the house, preparing the meals, shopping for food, or taking out the trash. Sometimes the scenery doesn't change much. While there are times we carve out and set aside time to escape the routine, like vacations, proportionally it's the mundane and repetitious "stuff" which makes up our days and ultimately our lives. We must learn to find joy and purpose in the daily grind or we risk compromising our finish - resist the urge to pack it in, slow down and listen for that quiet voice which reminds us to stay the course, keep the faith, and **BELIEVE** that it is all well worth the grind.

"I have fought the good fight. I have finished the course. I have kept the faith"

Confirmation or Contradiction

On the back of my car, I've got two symbols. The symbol on the left denotes the fact that I am an Ironman. The symbol on the right suggests that I am a Christian. Wherever I drive, people who see my car could rightly assume that I'm both fit and faithful. So here's the million dollar question. Am I living my life in such a way that people can see - not just by my words, but by my actions - that I am who I suggest I am?

It's pretty obvious that I walk the talk of an Ironman athlete. I train daily. I show for races I've committed to competing in, often preparing months in advance, without a day off, to ensure that I'm ready for the big event. People see me train, they see that fitness and wellness is a way of life for me, and they know that it's a passion of mine. I don't have to tell anybody that I'm a triathlete. I am because I do.

But is it so obvious that I am a Christian? Is my daily walk confirmation or a contradiction of my faith? Are my actions, my behaviors, my deeds aligned with Whom I suggest I follow? Just as people see that I am an athlete, a committed and dedicated competitor, through my daily pursuits on the road or in the gym, can they see that I am a committed and dedicated follower who is LIVING his purpose not just through words but through deeds?

THIS is my daily challenge. It's far easier for me to get my butt out of bed in the morning and train. I've been doing it religiously for 25+ years. But to move through each day *intentionally* living in a way which visibly demonstrates my faith and the love that I am called to share with others - even those who have hurt or wronged me? No easy task. But if my life is to be a confirmation of my faith, then I must. We must live in a way which attracts and does not repel others to the love and life in Jesus Christ. Our actions must align with our words. We must **live** the symbols which we claim represent us.

"You are the light of the world. A City on a hill cannot be hidden. Neither do people light a lamp and put it under a bowl. Instead, they put it on its stand, and it gives light to everyone in the house. In the same way, let your light shine before men, that they may see your good deeds and praise your Father in Heaven." - Matthew 5:14-16

Racing Ahead or Being Led

"Be still and Know that I am God" - Psalm 46:10

I'll admit it. I struggle with being still. I'm one of the most active, unstill, driven people around. I always have to be "doing" something. And yet I just spent a week alone, with no schedules, no planned activities, no conversations, and lots of "still" time. I did run on the beach and swim in the ocean, but aside from my early morning workouts I basically chilled - reading, napping, sitting, laying around. After a year of running full out, I stopped. And here's what I learned about myself.

I've not spent enough quiet time with God to recognize His voice when He speaks to me. I've been racing ahead instead of being led. Christian author and Pastor Jentezen Franklin describes what happens when we race ahead without slowing down and seeking God's will for our lives. In "*Right People, Right Place, Right Plan*", Franklin suggests that we can find ourselves "running at breakneck speed, confused, unproductive, always pushing and driving." That's me. The fall-out from racing ahead often isn't pretty. While we're doing it, we think we're making progress, getting things done, being hugely productive. And then something happens, mistakes are made as we rush through life, and sometimes we crash and burn.

So I slowed down long enough to recognize that I've been trying to force things to happen. I've been racing ahead - without knowing the course in advance. I've been doing the leading, instead of being still and seeking the discerning voice of God. Jesus spent considerable alone time with His Father, for good reason. In the quiet times, God speaks to us. We won't hear or learn anything if we are out racing ahead, pursuing our own agenda, assuming that we know what's best for us.

"Be still in the presence of the Lord, and wait for Him to act" - Psalm 37:7

It's time to get back to being led. It's time to apply the lessons learned from a week away and alone, to my life and daily walk. It's time to consciously carve out the quiet time each day to be still, be patient, and wait for God to act. It's time to truly **BELIEVE** that the God who created me, cares for me, and loves me more than I can imagine, knows what is best for me.

Everything Can Look Like Failure in the Middle

"Good morning athletes.....welcome to the start of a very long day. Recognize that you WILL have low points throughout this race, it may be at mile 85 of the bike or mile 21 on the run. But know this - you WILL get through those times, you WILL persevere, and we WILL see you back here crossing the finish line to welcome you all in as an **IRONMAN"**

So went the pre-race welcome as we awaited the start of 2010 Ironman Wisconsin in Madison. Treading the waters of Lake Monona for a good 15 minutes prior to the 2.4 mile swim, everyone has doubts. There isn't anyone 100% sure that the day will unfold they way they have planned, and that is part of the beauty of training for and competing in a long distance endurance event. At first I wondered why the announcer felt the need to remind all 3200 of us that we'd have some rough times along the way - after all, it seemed obvious and the way I saw it, we didn't need any additional reminders that what was about to unfold was no picnic. But the more I thought about it the more brilliant the comments seemed.

Preparing ourselves for difficult times or even failure, along the road to success, is a good thing. At the start of anything worthwhile or worth achieving, there is hope and optimism. You make a commitment by signing up for a race, you're fired up about the possibilities ahead, you begin to create this vision of achievement and success, of crossing the finish line - Mission Accomplished. The second phase is characterized by confidence - a "can-do" spirit fueled perhaps by past experience or the support of friends and family.

And then reality sets in. Invariably, somewhere along the way but typically in the middle, there will be emotional lows - negative thoughts and experiences that will cause us to question the endeavor and the decision to pursue the goal. It's not a matter of "if", but when. Whether it's week 12 of a 16 week Ironman training period or mile 85 of the 112 mile bike leg of the Ironman event itself, there WILL be those moments of angst and doubt, emotional and physical lows which one must push through. Knowing in advance that they WILL happen is a good thing. Creating this expectation of struggle and perhaps failure along the way is what authors Chip and Dan Heath call "The Growth Mindset". Although it seems to draw attention to failure, it reminds us of the road ahead...."We will struggle, we will fail, we will be knocked down - but throughout, we'll get better, and we WILL succeed in the end" (Switch: How to Change Things When Change is Hard).

So I have learned to embrace - going in - the fact that difficult times are bound to occur. I actually plan for them now - mentally and physically. No illusions. So that when they hit, I'm ready for them and am better able and more capable of dealing with what is to come...and pass. Paul's prayers to God on behalf of the Colossians asked simply for two things: Strength and Endurance. He knew tough times were ahead, and he prepared the Colossians for what was to come:

"May you be made strong with all the strength that comes from His glorious power, and may you be prepared to endure everything with patience, while joyfully giving thanks to the Father." (Colossians 1:11).

It's all about managing and changing our expectations - knowing going in that it won't be easy, the early euphoria will fade, the day will become long and the struggle hard. **Expect** the lows. *Expect* the roadblocks. *Expect* the rough patches. But *EXPECT* to come through it all, with the strength and endurance our Lord has ensured we can carry when we go it with Him. ***BELIEVE***.

Made in the USA
San Bernardino, CA
20 February 2014